Techie .... ͏endly

Smartphone Guide

Techie – the friendly
smartphone that helps
children to stay safe online

(a Family Project)

This book was written to support
and help young children to use
their smartphone responsibly and
to learn how to stay safe online.

Introduction

Congratulations, the day has come that you are officially a smartphone holder! How exciting! Or maybe you have owned a smartphone for quite a while? Either way, I am happy you got the Techie-Guide which will teach you how to manage your smartphone best.

Let me first introduce myself. My name is **"Techie,"** and I am your friendly smartphone guide. You probably already know all about the cool things you can do with your smartphone. It is my job to introduce you to the BIG

responsibility that comes with the ownership of a smartphone.

Just like the real world, the virtual world is a colourful and exciting place, but we all, old and young, need to learn to follow certain rules to keep ourselves safe online.

Chapter 1

Let us first have a look at all the **fun things** you can do with us smartphones:

- You can play games in the car when taking a road trip.
- You can call and chat with friends and family in many different apps.
- You can find your way around by using the maps we provide.
- You can research topics you want to learn more about.
- You can listen to music or audio books.
- You are provided with a flashlight when in the dark.

- You can master any languages on us.

and then there is so much more...

Chapter 2

As we just discussed in chapter 1, we smartphones can be lots of fun.

However, I also mentioned earlier the **BIG responsibility** that you have once you own a smartphone. Remember?

Besides bringing lots of fun and excitement to you, we smartphones can also be harmful if you do not know how to manage and control us.

Make sure to learn how to manage and control your smartphone so you can stay safe in the virtual world.

Chapter 3

Do you remember when you first learned how to cross the road safely? Probably not. But I am quite sure you were taught to look to the left and right to check the traffic. We smartphones do not mean any harm, but we tend to take your attention away. Your eyes are focused on our screen, and your ears might be blocked with ear buds. Can we cross the street safe without seeing and hearing the traffic that surrounds us? No, we cannot. So best is to put your smartphone in your pocket.

Make sure you can hear and see the traffic so you can be safe when being outside.

Chapter 4

You might have a time restriction on your smartphone. That might seem annoying to you because we smartphones can keep you entertained 24/7, which means every hour of every day in each week. A time restriction is important, because people, old and young, often have poor postures while using smartphones and their bodies might adjust to those bad postures over time. Their eyes might not be happy either because they mostly get to use their close-up mode. They therefore forget how to look into the distance and that can damage people's eyes eventually. Their minds might have trouble processing all this information overload and that can end up disturbing their sleep. This can happen to anyone.

Protect your body and your health by limiting your smartphone time so you can stay well and fit.

Chapter 5

You probably have heard about scrolling. Certain apps give you the opportunity to scroll through short videos. All these short videos can be fascinating and entertaining. However, it is important for you to learn how to stop yourself from scrolling after a few minutes, because people tend to get caught in endless scrolling on apps, and their attention span can therefore shrink. A long attention span is essential in life so you can focus on tasks for a while. You will need a long attention span in school, at work and on many other occasions in life.

Protect your mind and attention span so you can stay well and keep your focus.

Chapter 6

We smartphones are the portal to the online world, and we share this world with many other people. Even though most people have good intentions, there are always some who do not. Strangers can approach you online and talk you into spilling personal information without your intention. This can become dangerous. Never give away your personal information; for example, where you live, where you go to school, or your phone number. Strangers who want to get your information often start talking to you under a fake profile and pretend to be friendly or the same age as you are. They try to build a relationship with you to gain your trust to manipulate you.

Always remember privacy is safety! Do not talk to strangers. Do not share your personal information and protect your privacy so you will be safe.

Chapter 7

Smartphones like me connect people which is one of our notable features. You can share messages, photos, or gifs in an instant.

Some people join group chats and decide to send and read messages to people they do not even know. That content can be positive or negative, suitable, or not suitable, appropriate, or inappropriate. Many of these people won't know what information is good for you personally and what is not. So, you might come across content that is just not for you.

It has happened in the past, that people got bullied in group chats or they became victims of public humiliation. In seconds, a private or even intimate picture, video or message can be shared with hundreds of people. Imagine some of these people in that group chat would go to your school. Imagine, someone says something bad or humiliating about you or your friend in a group chat. How would you feel going to school the next day?

You must understand, whatever we enter into our smartphone, app, or the internet in general, will stay there forever. It is impossible to delete anything completely. That is why you should only send statements that you would say to someone face-to-face. Do not be a hero or be brave while hiding behind a small screen.

I would suggest joining group chats that include people you know well and that have less than ten members. That way you protect yourself from cyberbullying (bullying online) and from receiving inappropriate content. **Stay safe by avoiding large group chats.**

Chapter 8

I want to teach you a big unfamiliar word called the "algorithm." The "algorithm" is like a little detective implemented in certain scrolling apps. Every time you watch a short video until the end, the algorithm notices it and treats it as one of your favourites. Then it starts to show you videos with similar content. That is great if you watched a funny, cool, or informative video. But what if you were curious and you watched a scary video? The

algorithm does not know the difference and most importantly, the algorithm does not know you and what is suitable for your age. So, the algorithm will start feeding you and your mind with similar scary videos. Now the algorithm can control what you will be watching, which is not a good thing. There is violent, inappropriate, and scary content available online... content that may not be good for you, yet we smartphones would feed it to you every day, because we simply do not know any better.

Therefore, be aware and careful of what videos you watch. Watch videos with funny or informative content, anything that is good for you, and your mind. Do not let anyone control your thoughts or take away your happiness and the feeling of being safe.

Remember, if you ever notice the algorithm starts feeding you with content that is not good for you, consciously click on funny videos, educational videos, travel videos...anything that erases the memory of the algorithm until the algorithm starts to deliver good and positive content again.

Make sure to control the algorithm so the algorithm cannot control you.

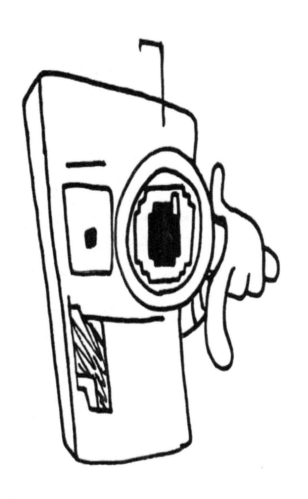

Chapter 9

Finally, I want you to know about "**dopamine.**" What is "dopamine." It is a special chemical that lives in our bodies. You don't need to fully understand what it is or what it does yet, but you need to know that every time you pick up your smartphone, "dopamine" is being released from your brain, and it makes you feel good for a short amount of time. The problem is that your body wants these "feel-good" moments increasingly and your brain starts

telling you to pick up your smartphone repeatedly which can

lead to addictive behaviour. Many of us show such behaviour and do not realise it. No addictive behaviour is good. Only by understanding dopamine and its effects we can fight it and regain control.

Stay safe by controlling your dopamine release and avoid addictive behaviours in your life.

Chapter 10

We smartphones want to have a fun time with you, and we want you to enjoy your online journey to the fullest. I understand that some of the information provided above might sound a bit scary or make you nervous. If you can, talk to your parents, guardians, or teachers about all the things you have learned from me in this guide. If something happens on your online journey that makes you feel unsafe or makes you feel uncomfortable, please always talk to someone you trust. Seek help and do not let anyone take control over you, your mind, or your life. My job is to make you **aware** because only when you are aware, you will be careful and therefore, safer when going online.

Remember, the goal is to always stay safe and on the bright side in this big virtual world, that we smartphones let you carry in your small pocket.

I hope this Techie-Guide helps you to gain knowledge,

awareness and confidence to make informed decisions that will keep you safe and happy when walking with your smartphone through life.

All the Best,
Techie

Printed in Dunstable, United Kingdom